'THE '30s

**MELODY LINE, CHORDS AND LYRICS
FOR KEYBOARD • GUITAR • VOCAL**

HAL•LEONARD®

ISBN 0-634-06416-9

Printed In Canada

HAL•LEONARD®
CORPORATION

7777 W. BLUEMOUND RD. P.O. BOX 13819 MILWAUKEE, WI 53213

Visit Hal Leonard Online at
www.halleonard.com

Welcome to the PAPERBACK SONGS SERIES.

Do you play piano, guitar, electronic keyboard, sing or play any instrument for that matter? If so, this handy "pocket tune" book is for you.

The concise, one-line music notation consists of:

MELODY, LYRICS & CHORD SYMBOLS

Whether strumming the chords on guitar, "faking" an arrangement on piano/keyboard or singing the lyrics, these fake book style arrangements can be enjoyed at any experience level – hobbyist to professional.

The musical skills necessary to successfully use this book are minimal. If you play guitar and need some help with chords, a basic chord chart is included at the back of the book.

While playing and singing is the first thing that comes to mind when using this book, it can also serve as a compact, comprehensive reference guide.

However you choose to use this PAPERBACK SONGS SERIES book, by all means have fun!

CONTENTS

(contents continued)

ALL OF ME

Words and Music by SEYMOUR SIMONS
and GERALD MARKS

Moderately

All of me ___ why not take all of me, ___ Can't you see ___ I'm no good with- out you? ___ Take my lips ___ I want to lose them, ___ Take my arms ___ I'll nev - er use

APRIL IN PARIS

Words by E.Y. HARBURG
Music by VERNON DUKE

Moderately

A-pril In Par- is, ___ chest-nuts in blos- som, ___ hol-i-day ta- bles un-der the trees. ___ A-pril In Par- is, ___ this is a feel- ing ___ no one can ev- er ___ re- prise. ___

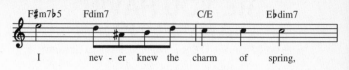

I never knew the charm of spring,

nev - er met it face to face.

I never knew my heart could sing,

nev - er missed a warm em - brace, till

A - pril In Par - is, _____

whom can I turn to, _____ what have you done to __

__ my heart? _____

ARE YOU HAVIN' ANY FUN?

from GEORGE WHITE'S SCANDALS (1939 Edition)

Words by JACK YELLEN
Music by SAMMY FAIN

14

BEER BARREL POLKA
(Roll Out the Barrel)
Based on the European success "Skoda Lasky"*

By LEW BROWN, WLADIMIR A. TIMM,
JAROMIR VEJVODA and VASEK ZEMAN

There's a gar - den, what a gar - den, On - ly

hap - py fa - ces bloom there And there's nev - er an - y

room there For a wor - ry or a

gloom there Oh! there's mu - sic and there's

danc - ing And a lot of sweet ro -

manc - ing When they play a

pol - ka They all get in the

16

AT LONG LAST LOVE

Words and Music by
COLE PORTER

Slowly

Is it an earth - quake_____ or sim - ply a

shock?_____ Is it the good tur - tle soup

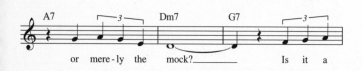

or mere - ly the mock?_____ Is it a

cock - tail,_____ this feel - ing of joy,_____

_____ Or is what I feel the real Mc - Coy?_____

Is it for all time,_____ or sim-ply a

lark?_____ Is it Gra - na - da I see or

on - ly As -bur - y Park?_____ Is it a

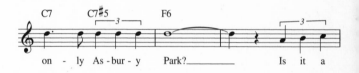

fan - cy_____ not worth think - ing of,_____

_____ or is it at long last

love?_____ Is it an   love?_____

BETWEEN THE DEVIL AND THE DEEP BLUE SEA

from RHYTHMANIA

Lyric by TED KOEHLER
Music by HAROLD ARLEN

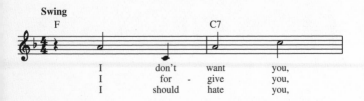

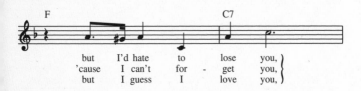

I ought to cross you off my list, ___

but when you come knock - ing at my door, ___

fate seems to give my heart a twist, ___ and

D.C. al Coda

I come run - ning back for more.

CODA

dev - il and the deep blue sea. ___

BEYOND THE BLUE HORIZON

from the Paramount Picture MONTE CARLO

Words by LEO ROBIN
Music by RICHARD A. WHITING and W. FRANKE HARLING

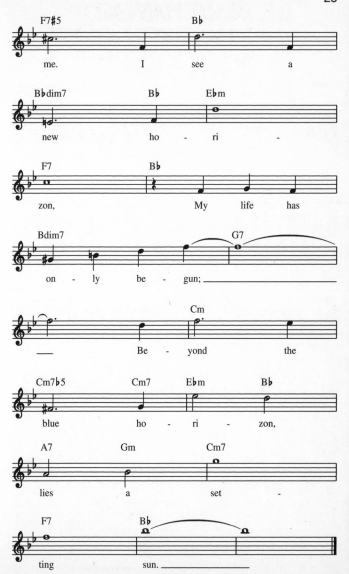

BLUE HAWAII

from the Paramount Picture WAIKIKI WEDDING

Words and Music by LEO ROBIN
and RALPH RAINGER

Slowly

Night and you and Blue Ha - wa - ii,

the night is heav - en - ly and _ you are

heav - en to me. _____ Love - ly you

and Blue Ha - wa - ii, with all this

love - li - ness there _ should be love. _____

Come with me _____ while the

moon is on the sea. _____ The night is young _____

_____ and so are we. _____

Dreams come true in Blue Ha - wa - ii

and mine could all come true this _ mag - ic

night of nights with you. you.

BODY AND SOUL

Words by EDWARD HEYMAN, ROBERT SOUR and FRANK EYTON
Music by JOHN GREEN

Expressively

hard to con-ceive it that you'd turn a-way ro - mance. _

Are you pre-tend-ing? It looks like the end-ing un -

less I could have one more dance to prove, dear.

My life a wreck you're mak - ing,

you know I'm yours for just the tak-ing; I'd glad-ly sur-

ren - der my-self to you, bod-y and

soul!   soul!

BOO-HOO

Lyric and Music by EDWARD HEYMAN,
CARMEN LOMBARDO and JOHN JACOB LOEB

BY MYSELF
from BETWEEN THE DEVIL

Words by HOWARD DIETZ
Music by ARTHUR SCHWARTZ

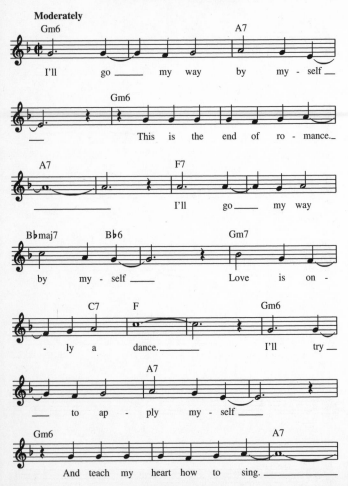

BYE BYE BLUES

**Words and Music by FRED HAMM, DAVE BENNETT
BERT LOWN and CHAUNCEY GRAY**

CHEEK TO CHEEK

from the RKO Radio Motion Picture TOP HAT

Words and Music by
IRVING BERLIN

34

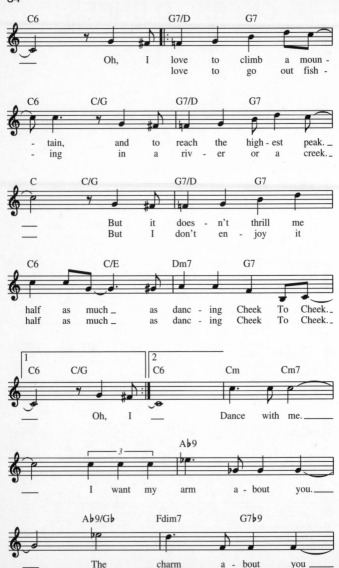

CARAVAN

Words and Music by DUKE ELLINGTON,
IRVING MILLS and JUAN TIZOL

Dbdim	C7	Fm6

on our car - a - van. _____
of our car - a - van. _____
des - ert car - a - van. _____

Fine

F7   F7b9

This _____ is so ex - cit -

F+   Bb7

ing, you _____ are so in -

Fm7/Bb   Bb7   Eb7

vit - ing rest - ing in my

Gdim7   Ab

arms as I thrill to _____

D.C. al Fine

C7 Fm6/C Cdim7 C7

_____ the mag - ic charms _____ of

CARELESS

**Words and Music by LEW QUADLING,
EDDY HOWARD and DICK JERGENS**

THE CHAMPAGNE WALTZ

Theme from the Paramount Picture
THE CHAMPAGNE WALTZ

Words and Music by CON CONRAD,
BEN OAKLAND and MILTON DRAKE

CHEROKEE
(Indian Love Song)

Words and Music by
RAY NOBLE

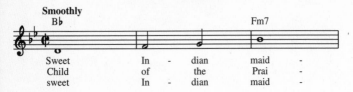

Sweet
Child
sweet

In
of
In

dian
the
dian

maid -
Prai -
maid -

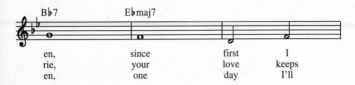

en,
rie,
en,

since
your
one

first
love
day

I
keeps
I'll

met
call -
hold

you,
ing,
you,

I
my
in

To Coda ⊕

can't
heart
my

for -
en -
arms

get
thrall -
fold

you,
ing,
you,

Cher -
Cher -

o -
kee

sweet -

heart.

o -

kee. _____ Dreams _____ of

sum - mer - time, _____ of lov - er - time _____

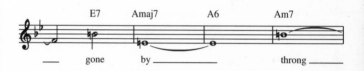

_____ gone by _____ throng _____

_____ my mem - o - ry _____ so

D.C. al Coda

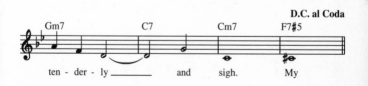

ten - der - ly _____ and sigh. My

CODA

Cher - o - kee. _____

COCKTAILS FOR TWO
from the Paramount Picture MURDER AT THE VANITIES

**Words and Music by ARTHUR JOHNSTON
and SAM COSLOW**

45

but my heart will be o - be - di - ent

with in - tox - i - cat - ing kiss - es ___ for the

prin - ci - ple in - gre - di - ent;

Most an - y af - ter - noon at five ___

___ we'll be so glad we're both a - live. ___

Then may - be for - tune will com - plete her plan, that

Dm7   G7   C6   Fm   C

all be - gan with cock - tails for two. ___

DANCING ON THE CEILING

from SIMPLE SIMON

Words by LORENZ HART
Music by RICHARD RODGERS

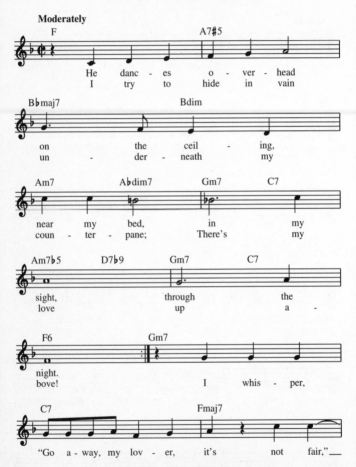

Am7b5   D7   Gm7

_____   but   I'm   so

C7

grate - ful   to   dis - cov - er

F   F#dim7   Gm7   C7

he's   still   there. _____

F   A7#5

I   love   my   ceil - ing   more

Bbmaj7   Bdim   Am7   Abdim7

since   it   is   a   danc - ing   floor

Gm7   C7

just   for _____   my

F

love. _____

DID YOU EVER SEE A DREAM WALKING?

from SITTING PRETTY

Words by MACK GORDON
Music by HARRY REVEL

Did you ev-er see a dream walk-ing? Well, I did! _____ Did you ev-er hear a dream talk-ing? Well, I did! _____ Did you ev-er have a dream thrill you with "Will you be mine?" _____ Oh, it's so grand _____ and it's too, too di-vine. _____ Did you ev-er see a dream

EAST OF THE SUN
(And West of the Moon)

Words and Music by
BROOKS BOWMAN

East of the sun _____ and west of the moon, ___ We'll build a dream-house _____ of love, dear. Near to the sun in the day, near to the moon at night we'll live in a love-ly way, dear, Liv-ing on love and pale moon-light. Just you and I, _____ for -

EASTER PARADE

featured in the Motion Picture
Irving Berlin's EASTER PARADE

Words and Music by
IRVING BERLIN

EASY TO LOVE
(You'd Be So Easy to Love)
from BORN TO DANCE

Words and Music by
COLE PORTER

EXACTLY LIKE YOU

Words by DOROTHY FIELDS
Music by JIMMY McHUGH

FALLING IN LOVE WITH LOVE

from THE BOYS FROM SYRACUSE

Words by LORENZ HART
Music by RICHARD RODGERS

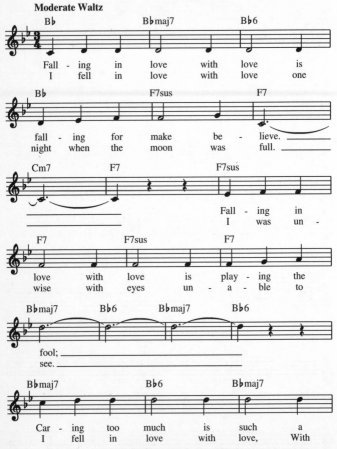

A FINE ROMANCE
from SWING TIME

Words by DOROTHY FIELDS
Music by JEROME KERN

FOR ALL WE KNOW

Words by SAM M. LEWIS
Music by J. FRED COOTS

FRIENDSHIP

from DUBARRY WAS A LADY

Words and Music by
COLE PORTER

66

I CAN'T GET
STARTED WITH YOU

from ZIEGFELD FOLLIES

Words by IRA GERSHWIN
Music by VERNON DUKE

mov - ies want _ me to star; I've got a
ads all fea - ture my smiles; the As - tor -

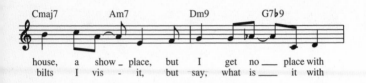

house, a show _ place, but I get no _ place with
bilts I vis - it, but say, what is _ it with

you. You're so su -
you? When we first

preme, lyr - ics I write _ of you,
met, how you e - lat - ed me!

scheme just for a sight _ of you,
Pet, you dev - as - tat - ed me!

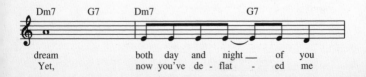

dream both day and night _ of you
Yet, now you've de - flat - ed me

Em11   A9   D9   G7 N.C.

and   what   good does   it do? In nine-teen
'til   you're   my Wa - ter-loo. I've sold my

Cmaj7   Am7   Dm9   G7

twen - ty-nine __ I sold   short, _____ in Eng-land
kiss - es   at __ a ba - zaar, _____ and af - ter

Bm7 E7 Bbm9 Eb9#11 D9   G9

I'm pre - sent - ed at court,   but you've got
me they've named _ a ci - gar;   but late - ly

Cmaj7   A7#5   Dm9   G9

me down-heart - ed 'cause I can't get start - ed with
how I've smart - ed, 'cause I can't get start - ed with

1
C6   A7#5   D9   G9 N.C.

you.   I do a

2
C6   F9   C6/9

you. _____

GET OUT OF TOWN

Words and Music by
COLE PORTER

Moderately

Get out of town_ Be - fore_ it's too

late, my love;_ Get out of town,_

Be good_ to me, please._

Why wish me harm?_ Why not re - tire to a farm_

And be con - tent - ed to charm_ The birds_ off the

trees?_____ Just dis-ap-pear,_

I care_ for you much too much,_ And

when you are near,_ Close to me, dear,_ We

touch too much._ The thrill when we meet is

so bit-ter-sweet That, dar-ling, it's get-ting me down._

___ So on your mark,_ get set, Get out of

town._____   town._____

THE GLORY OF LOVE

Words and Music by
BILLY HILL

You've got to give a lit-tle, take a lit-tle and let your poor heart break a lit-tle that's the sto-ry of, that's the glo-ry of love. _____ You've got to laugh a lit-tle cry a lit-tle be-fore the clouds roll by a lit-tle that's the sto-ry of, that's the glo-ry of love. _____ As long as there's the

GOT A DATE
WITH AN ANGEL
from FOR THE LOVE OF MIKE

Words by CLIFFORD GREY and SONNY MILLER
Music by JACK WALLER and JOSEPH TURNBRIDGE

Heav - en.   Soon I'll hear the bells   ring   out,

And   the cho - ir will   sing   out,

when the pearl - y gates swing out   She'll beck - on   to

me.   I've been wait - ing a   life - time,

For   this eve - ning at   sev - en,

Got   a date   with an   an - gel   And

I'm   on   my   way   to   Heav - en.   Heav - en.

HARBOR LIGHTS

Words and Music by JIMMY KENNEDY
and HUGH WILLIAMS

77

HAVE YOU EVER BEEN LONELY?

(Have You Ever Been Blue?)

Words by GEORGE BROWN
Music by PETER DeROSE

Moderately

F/C C

Have you ev-er been lone - ly? _____ Have you ev-er been

G7

blue? _____ Have you ev-er loved

some - one _____ just as I love you? _____

C   C7   F   F#dim7

_____ Can't you see I'm sor - ry _____ for each mis-take I've

C   G7   C   Eb7   G   G#dim7

made? _____ Can't you see I've changed, dear, _____

D7   Dm7   G7

_____ can't you see I've paid? _____ Be a lit - tle for -

HAVE YOU MET MISS JONES?

from I'D RATHER BE RIGHT

Words by LORENZ HART
Music by RICHARD RODGERS

HEART AND SOUL

from the Paramount Short Subject A SONG IS BORN

Words and FRANK LOESSER
Music by HOAGY CARMICHAEL

HEARTACHES

Words by JOHN KLENNER
Music by AL HOFFMAN

HEAT WAVE

from the Stage Production AS THOUSANDS CHEER

Words and Music by
IRVING BERLIN

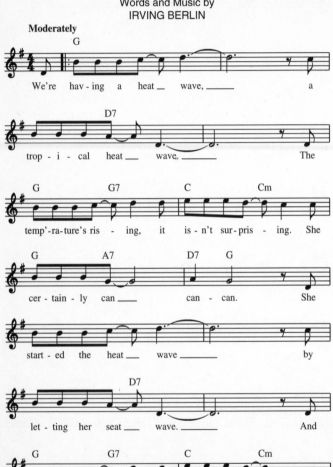

We're hav-ing a heat __ wave, ____ a

trop-i-cal heat __ wave. ____ The

temp'-ra-ture's ris - ing, it is-n't sur-pris - ing. She

cer-tain-ly can __ can - can. She

start-ed the heat __ wave by

let-ting her seat __ wave. ____ And

in such a way __ that the cus-tom-ers say __ that she

cer - tain - ly can __ can can. Gee __

__ her __ a - na - to - my __

__ made __ the mer - cur - y __

__ jump __ to nine - ty three. Yes sir! __ We're

hav - ing a heat __ wave, __ a

trop - i - cal heat __ wave. __ The

way that she moves __ that ther - mo - me - ter proves __ that she

cer - tain - ly can __ can can. We're can - can.

HOW DEEP IS THE OCEAN
(How High Is the Sky)

Words and Music by
IRVING BERLIN

Slowly

How much do I love you?

I'll tell you no lie.

How Deep Is The O - cean,

how high is the sky?

How man - y times a day __ do

I think of you? __ How man - y ros -

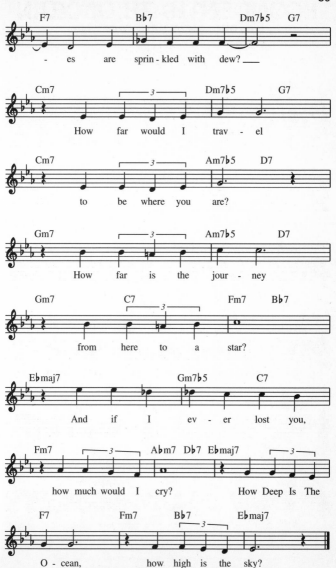

I CONCENTRATE ON YOU
from BROADWAY MELODY OF 1940

Words and Music by
COLE PORTER

Slowly

When-ev-er skies look grey to me ___

and trou-ble be -

gins to brew, ___

when-ev-er the win-ter winds

be-come too strong, I con-cen -

trate on you. ___

When for - tune cries, "Nay, nay!" to me ____

____ and peo - ple de -

clare, "You're through," ____

when - ev - er the blues be - come

my on - ly song,

I con - cen - trate on you. ____

____ On your smile so sweet, so

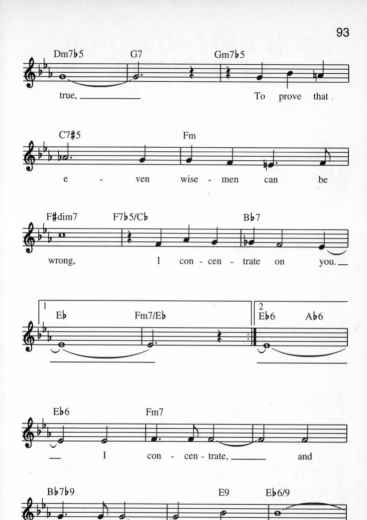

true, _____ To prove that

even wise - men can be

wrong, I con - cen - trate on you. __

I con - cen - trate, _____ and

con - cen - trate _____ on you. __

I DON'T STAND A GHOST OF A CHANCE

Words by BING CROSBY and NED WASHINGTON
Music by VICTOR YOUNG

G7 ... **G7♯5**

If you'd sur-ren-der   Just for a ten-der

C ... **Am6**

kiss or two,_____   You might dis-cov-er,

B7 ... **E9**

that I'm the lov-er   meant for you, And

G7♯5 ... **C**

I'd be true, But what's the good of

G+ **Em7♭5** **A7** **Fm6**

schem-ing, I know I must be dream-ing, For

C **Am** **D7** **G7♯5** | **1.** **C** **A♭7**

I don't stand a ghost of a chance with you!_____

D7 **G7♯5** | **2.** **C** **F9** **C6**

__ I you! _____

I FOUND A MILLION DOLLAR BABY
(In a Five and Ten Cent Store)

Lyric by BILLY ROSE and MORT DIXON
Music by HARRY WARREN

It was a luck - y A - pril show - er,

it was the most con - ve - nient door

I found a mil - lion dol - lar ba - by in a

five and ten cent store; The rain con-tin - ued for an

hour, I hung a-round for three or four,

a-round a mil - lion dol - lar ba - by in a

five and ten cent store. She was sell - ing

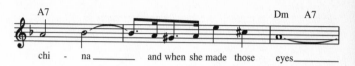

chi - na _____ and when she made those eyes_____

_____ I kept buy - ing chi - na _____ un-til the crowd got

wise. _____ In - ci - den - t'ly, if you should run in-to a

show - er, just step in-side my cot - tage door

and meet the mil - lion dol - lar ba - by from the

five and ten cent store! store!

I WON'T DANCE
from ROBERTA

Words and Music by JIMMY McHUGH, DOROTHY FIELDS,
JEROME KERN, OSCAR HAMMERSTEIN II and OTTO HARBACH

I'LL BE SEEING YOU

from RIGHT THIS WAY

Lyric by IRVING KAHAL
Music by SAMMY FAIN

Freely, rubato

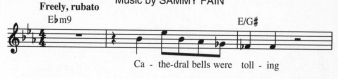

Ca - the-dral bells were toll - ing

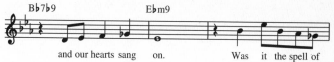

and our hearts sang on. Was it the spell of

Par - is or the A - pril dawn? Who knows

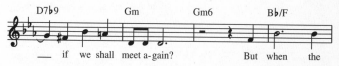

if we shall meet a-gain? But when the

morn - ing chimes ring sweet a - gain, I'll be

see-ing you in all the old fa - mil - iar plac - es

that this heart of mine em-brac - es all day through.

102

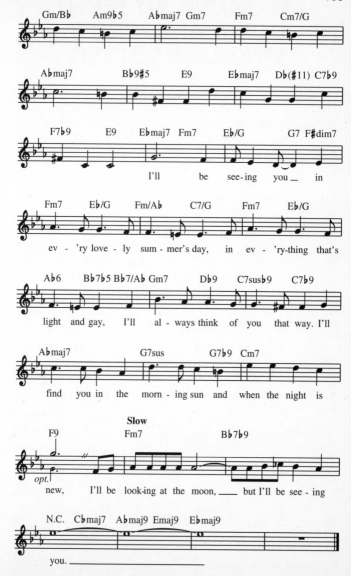

I'M GONNA SIT RIGHT DOWN AND WRITE MYSELF A LETTER

Lyric by JOE YOUNG
Music by FRED E. AHLERT

Moderately, with a lift

I'm gon-na sit right down and write my-self a let-ter _____ and make be-lieve it came from you. _____ I'm gon-na write words, oh, so sweet, they're gon-na knock me off my feet. A lot of kiss-es on the bot-tom, I'll be glad I

I'M PUTTING ALL MY EGGS IN ONE BASKET

from the Motion Picture FOLLOW THE FLEET

Words and Music by
IRVING BERLIN

Moderately

I've been a roam — ing { Ro - me - o,___ }
{ Ju - li - et,___ } my

{ Ju - li - ets___ } have been man - y.___
{ Ro me - os___ } But now my

roam-ing days___ have gone.___

Too man - y i - rons in the fire___ is

worse than not___ hav-ing an - y.___ I've had my

share and   from   now   on

I'm   put-ting   all   my   eggs   in   one

bas-ket.   I'm bet-ting ev - 'ry-thing I've got on   you.

    I'm   giv-ing   all

    my   love   to   one   ba - by.

Lord   help   me   if   my ba - by don't come   through.

I'VE GOT YOU UNDER MY SKIN

from BORN TO DANCE

Words and Music by
COLE PORTER

Moderately

Fm7   Bb7   Ebmaj7

I've got you _____ un-der my skin, _____

Cm7   Fm7   Bb7

_____ I've got you _____ deep in the

Ebmaj7   Cm7   Fm7

heart of me, _____ so deep in my heart, _____

Bb7   Ebmaj7   Cm7

_____ you're real-ly a part of me. I've

Fm7   Bb7   Ebmaj7

got you _____ un-der my skin. _____

Eb6   Fm7   Bb7

_____ I tried so _____ not to give

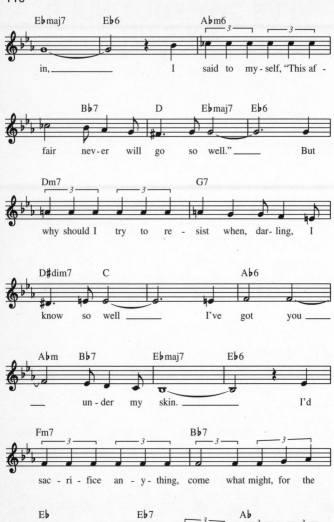

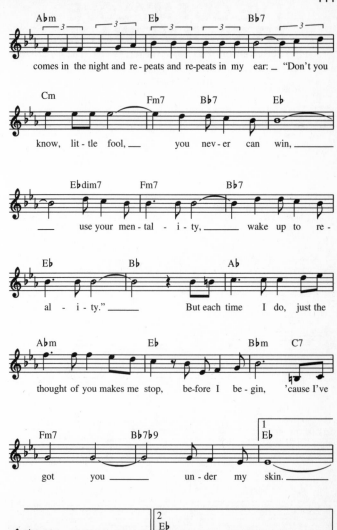

I'VE GOT MY LOVE
TO KEEP ME WARM

from the 20th Century Fox Motion Picture ON THE AVENUE

Words and Music by
IRVING BERLIN

The snow is snow-ing, the wind is
can't re-mem-ber a worse De -

blow-ing, but I can weath-er the storm.
cem-ber; just watch those i-ci-cles form.

What do I care how
What do I care if

much it may storm?
i-ci-cles form?

I've got my love to keep me warm.

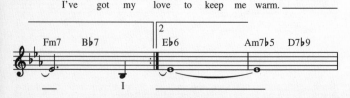

I'VE GOT THE WORLD ON A STRING

Lyric by TED KOEHLER
Music by HAROLD ARLEN

IN A SENTIMENTAL MOOD

Words and Music by DUKE ELLINGTON,
IRVING MILLS and MANNY KURTZ

par - a - dise com - plete.

Rose pet - als seem to fall, it's all like a dream to call you

mine. My heart's a light-er thing since

you make this night a thing di - vine.

In a sen - ti - men - tal mood

I'm with - in a world so heav - en - ly,

for I nev - er dreamt that you'd be lov - ing

sen - ti - men - tal me.

IN A SHANTY IN OLD SHANTY TOWN

Lyric by JOE YOUNG
Music by JACK LITTLE and IRA SCHUSTER

IN THE CHAPEL
IN THE MOONLIGHT

Words and Music by
BILLY HILL

How I'd love to hear the or - gan ___

___ in the chap - el in the moon - light ___

___ while we're stroll - ing down the aisle ___

___ where ros - es en - twine. ___

___ How I'd love to hear you

whis - per ___ in the chap - el in the

moon - light _____ that the love-light in your

eyes _____ for - ev - er will

shine _____ till the

ros - es turn to ash - es till the

or - gan turns to

rust if you nev - er come I'll

still be there till the

IN THE STILL OF THE NIGHT

from ROSALIE

Words and Music by
COLE PORTER

Moderately

In the still of the night,

as I gaze from my

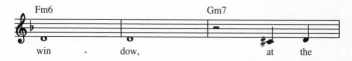

win - dow, at the

moon in its flight, my thoughts all

stray to you.

In the still of the

night, while the

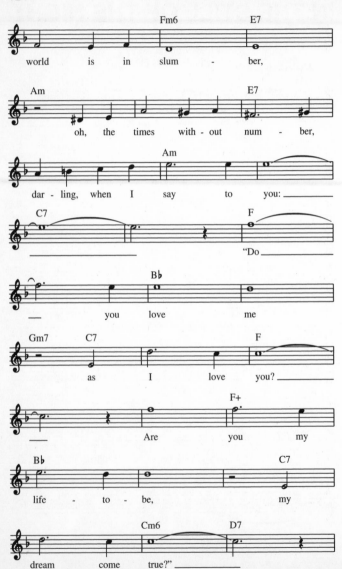

world   is   in   slum - ber,

Am / E7
oh,   the   times   with - out   num - ber,

Am
dar - ling,   when   I   say   to   you: _____

C7 / F
"Do _____

Bb
_____   you   love   me

Gm7   C7 / F
as   I   love   you? _____

F+
_____   Are   you   my

Bb / C7
life - to - be,   my

Cm6   D7
dream   come   true?" _____

IN THE MOOD

By JOE GARLAND

Moderate Swing

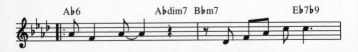

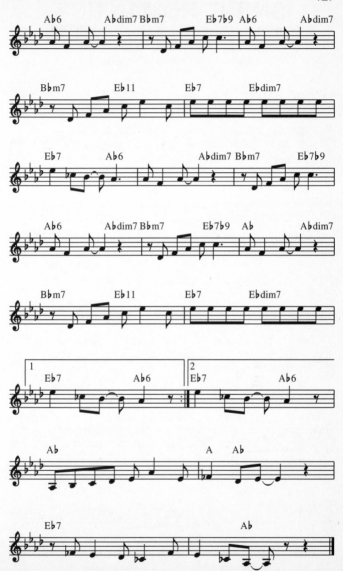

ISN'T IT ROMANTIC?

from the Paramount Picture LOVE ME TONIGHT

Words by LORENZ HART
Music by RICHARD RODGERS

129

IT DON'T MEAN A THING

(If It Ain't Got That Swing)
from SOPHISTICATED LADIES

Words and Music by DUKE ELLINGTON
and IRVING MILLS

wah.　　　It　　makes　　no　　dif - f'rence　if ___

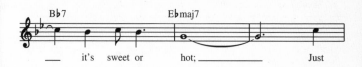

__　it's　sweet　or　　hot; _____　Just

give　that　rhy - thm　ev - 'ry - thing you

got.　　　　It　don't　mean　a

thing　　if　　it　　ain't　got that　swing, _

doo　wah, _　doo wah,　doo wah,　doo wah,　doo　wah,_

_　doo wah,　doo wah,　doo　wah.

IT'S A BLUE WORLD

Words and Music by BOB WRIGHT
and CHET FORREST

IT'S DE-LOVELY
from RED, HOT AND BLUE!

Words and Music by
COLE PORTER

Moderately

The night is young,_ The skies are clear _ And

if you want_ to go walk-ing, dear, It's de-light-ful,_ it's de-

li - cious,_ it's de-love - ly. _ I

un-der-stand_ the reas-on why_ You're sen-ti-men - tal, 'cause

so am I,_ It's de-light - ful,_ it's de - li - cious,_ it's de-

love - ly. _ You can tell at a glance

Bb   F7 F+   Bb

What a swell night this is for ro-mance, You can

Bbm6   C7

hear dear Moth-er Na-ture mur-mur-ing low,___ "Let your-

F   F+

-self go."_ So please be sweet,_ my chick-a-dee,_ And

F   F+ F

when I kiss_ you, just say to me,_ "It's de-light-ful,_ it's de-

F/E   Am7b5/Eb   D7

li - cious,, It's de-lect-a-ble,_ it's de-lir-i-ous,_ It's di-

G7/Db   C7   1. Gm/F F

lem-ma, it's_ de-li-mit, It's de-luxe, it's de-love-ly."___

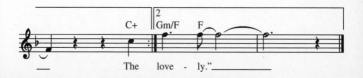

               C+   2. Gm/F F

___ The love-ly."___

IT'S EASY TO REMEMBER

from the Paramount Picture MISSISSIPPI

Words by LORENZ HART
Music by RICHARD RODGERS

fin - gers press me tight. _____ I'd rath - er

dream _____ than have that lone - ly feel - ing

steal - ing through the night. _____ Each lit - tle

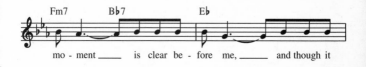

mo - ment _____ is clear be - fore me, _____ and though it

brings me re - gret, it's

eas - y to re - mem - ber, and

so hard to for - get.

IT'S ONLY A PAPER MOON

Lyric by BILLY ROSE and E.Y. HARBURG
Music by HAROLD ARLEN

IT'S THE TALK
OF THE TOWN

Words by MARTY SYMES and AL NEIBURG
Music by JERRY LIVINGSTON

Slowly, with expression

I can't show my face, can't go an-y-place,
Ev-'ry-time we meet, my heart skips a beat,

peo-ple stop and stare it's so hard to bear.
we don't stop to speak, tho' it's just a week.

Ev-'ry-bod-y knows you left me,

1 it's the talk of the town.

2 it's the talk of the town. We

sent out in-vi-ta-tions to friends and re-la-tions an-

141

JUST A GIGOLO

Original German Text by JULIUS BRAMMER
English Words by IRVING CAESAR
Music by LEONELLO CASUCCI

Moderately

Just a gig-o-lo, ev-'ry-where I go,
Schö-ner Gig-o-lo, ar-mer Gig-o-lo,

peo-ple know the part I'm play-ing. Paid for ev-'ry dance,
den-ke nicht mehr an die Zei-ten. Wo du als Hu-sar,

sell-ing each ro-mance, ev-'ry night some heart be-
gold-ver-schnürt so-gar, koon-test durch die Stras-sen

tray-ing. There will come a day, youth will pass a-way,
rei-ten! U-ni-form pas-sée, Lieb-chen sagt: A-dieu!

then what will they say a-bout ___ me. When the
Schö-ne Welt, du gingst in Fran-sen! Wenn das

end comes I know they'll say, "Just a gig-o-lo." As
Herz das auch bricht, zeig' ein Ja-chen-des Ge-sicht, man

life goes on with-out me.
zahit und du musst

tan-zen!

LET'S FACE THE MUSIC AND DANCE

from the Motion Picture FOLLOW THE FLEET

Words and Music by
IRVING BERLIN

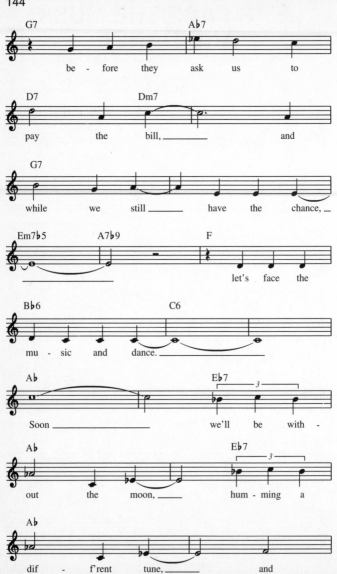

JUST ONE MORE CHANCE

Words by SAM COSLOW
Music by ARTHUR JOHNSTON

Moderately slow

Just One More Chance,— to prove it's you a-lone I care for, each night I say a lit-tle prayer for Just One More Chance.— Just one more night,— to taste the kiss-es that en-chant me, I'd want no oth-ers if you'd grant me Just One More Chance. —

THE LADY IS A TRAMP

from *BABES IN ARMS*

Words by LORENZ HART
Music by RICHARD RODGERS

Moderately bright

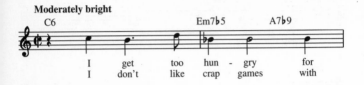

din - ner at eight. ____
bar - ons and earls. ____

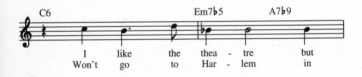

nev - er come late. ____
er - mine and pearls. ____

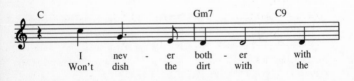

149

LET'S DANCE

Words by FANNY BALDRIDGE
Music by GREGORY STONE and JOSEPH BONINE

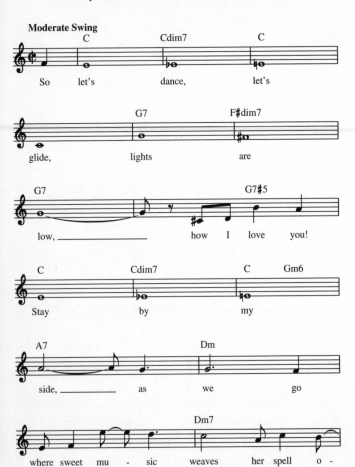

- ver   us.   Your

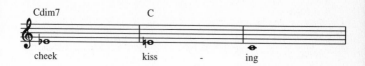

cheek   kiss - ing

mine,   my   sweet,

thrills   me   through, _ dear.   Ah!

Sweet   mel - o - dy,

come   guide   our   feet;

let's   dance. _____

LET'S HAVE ANOTHER CUP O' COFFEE

from the Stage Production FACE THE MUSIC

Words and Music by
IRVING BERLIN

LIFE IS JUST A BOWL
OF CHERRIES

from GEORGE WHITE'S SCANDALS (1931 Edition)

**Words and Music by LEW BROWN
and RAY HENDERSON**

Moderately

Life   is   just   a bowl   of cher - ries.___ Don't make   it

se - ri - ous.___ Life's too mys - te - ri - ous.___ You work, you save, you

wor - ry   so, But you can't take your dough when you go, go, go, So

keep   re - peat - ing, "It's the ber - ries." The   strong - est   oak must

fall.___ The sweet things in life, To you were just loaned_ so

how can you lose_ what you've nev - er owned.___ Life   is   just a bowl of

cher - ries, So   live   and laugh at it   all.

LOVELY TO LOOK AT
from ROBERTA

Words and Music by JIMMY McHUGH,
DOROTHY FIELDS and JEROME KERN

Love-ly to look at, de-light-ful to know and

heav-en to kiss. A com-bi-na-tion like this

— is quite my most im-pos-si-ble scheme come true. I-

mag-ine find-ing a dream like you! You're love-ly to look at. It's

thrill-ing to hold you ter-ri-bly tight. _____

— For we're to-geth-er, the moon is new, and

oh, it's love-ly to look at you to-night!_____

LITTLE GIRL BLUE

from JUMBO

Words by LORENZ HART
Music by RICHARD RODGERS

Moderately

Sit there and count your fin - gers
Sit there and count the rain - drops

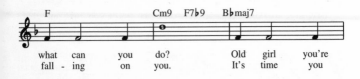

what can you do? Old girl you're
fall - ing on you. It's time you

through. Sit there and
knew, all you can

count your lit - tle fin - gers; un -
count on is the rain - drops that

luck - y Lit - tle Girl Blue. _____
fall on Lit - tle Girl Blue. _____

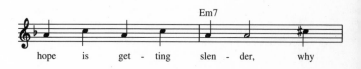

No use, old girl you may as well sur - ren - der, your hope is get - ting slen - der, why won't some - bod - y send a ten - der blue boy to cheer a Lit - tle Girl Blue?

LOVE IS THE SWEETEST THING

Words and Music by
RAY NOBLE

LOVER
from the Paramount Picture LOVE ME TONIGHT

Lyrics by LORENZ HART
Music by RICHARD RODGERS

THE MOST BEAUTIFUL GIRL IN THE WORLD

from JUMBO

Words by LORENZ HART
Music by RICHARD RODGERS

The most beau – ti – ful girl in the

world _____ Picks my ties out. _____

_____ Eats my can – dy.

_____ Drinks my bran – dy, _____

_____ the most beau – ti – ful girl in the

world! _____

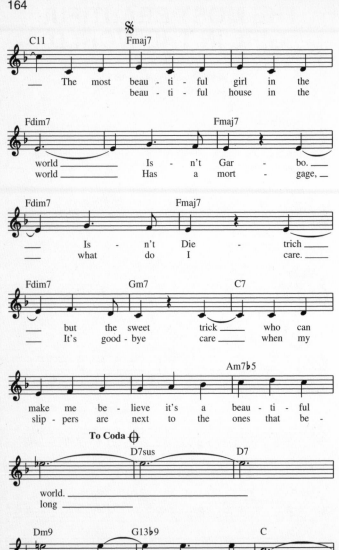

165

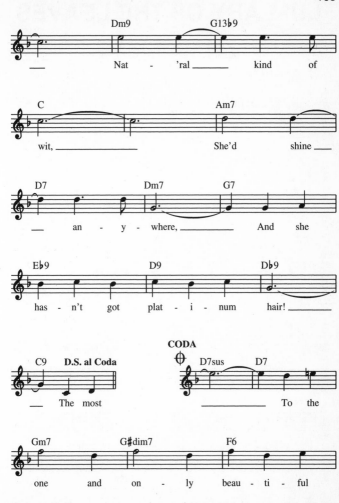

LULLABY OF THE LEAVES

Words by JOE YOUNG
Music by BERNICE PETKERE

Moderately

Cra - dle me where south - ern skies can

watch me with a mil - lion eyes. Oh,

sing me to sleep, lull - a - by of the

leaves. _____ Cov - er me with heav-en's blue and

let me dream a dream or two. Oh,

sing me to sleep, lull - a - by of the leaves.

MEMORIES OF YOU

Lyric by ANDY RAZAF
Music by EUBIE BLAKE

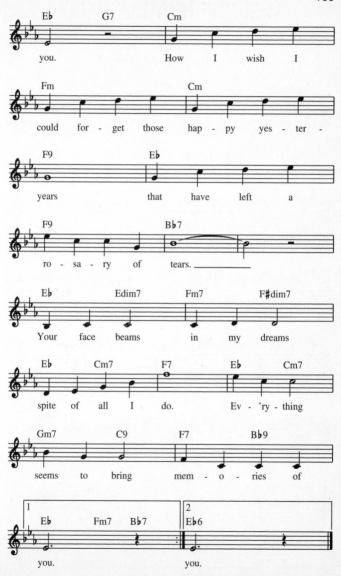

MIMI

from the Paramount Picture LOVE ME TONIGHT

Words by LORENZ HART
Music by RICHARD RODGERS

Cheerfully

Mi - mi, you

fun - ny lit - tle good for noth - ing

Mi - mi, am I the guy?

Mi - mi, you

sun - ny lit - tle hon - ey of a

Mi - mi, I'm aim - ing

high! _____ Mi - mi,

you've got me sad and dream - y,

you could free ___ me, if you'd see ___

___ me, Mi - mi,

you know I'd like to

have a lit - tle son of a

Mi - mi bye and bye. _____

MOOD INDIGO

Words and Music by DUKE ELLINGTON,
IRVING MILLS and ALBANY BIGARD

MOON OVER MIAMI

Lyric by EDGAR LESLIE
Music by JOE BURKE

hark to the throb - bing gui - tars.

Hear how the waves of - fer thun - der-ous ap - plause, _

af – ter each song to the stars.

Moon o - ver Mi - a - mi,

you know we're wait - ing for,_____ a lit - tle

love,_____ a lit - tle kiss on Mi -

a - mi shore.

MOONGLOW

Words and Music by WILL HUDSON, EDDIE DE LANGE and IRVING MILLS

Smoothly

It must have been Moon - glow,

way up in the blue,

it must have been Moon - glow

that led me straight to you; ___

I still hear you say - ing,

"Dear one, hold me fast."

And I start in pray - ing,

MY FUNNY VALENTINE

from BABES IN ARMS

Words by LORENZ HART
Music by RICHARD RODGERS

Slowly

My fun-ny val-en-tine, sweet com-ic

val-en-tine, you make me smile with my

heart. _____ Your looks are laugh-a-ble,

un-pho-to-graph-a-ble, yet, you're my

fav-'rite work of art. _____ Is your

MY HEART BELONGS TO DADDY

from LEAVE IT TO ME

Words and Music by
COLE PORTER

While tear-ing off __ a game of golf __ I may make a play for the cad-dy; but when I do __ I don't fol-low through __ 'cause my heart be-longs __ to dad-dy. If I in-vite __ a boy some night __ to dine on my fine fin-nan had-die, I just a-dore __ his ask-ing for more, __ but my

MY IDEAL
from the Paramount Picture PLAYBOY OF PARIS

Words by LEO ROBIN
Music by RICHARD A. WHITING and NEWELL CHASE

Slowly

Will I ev - er find the

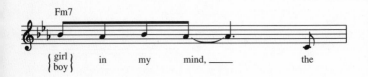

{ girl / boy } in my mind, _____ the

one who is my ____ i - deal?

May - be { she's / he's } a dream and

yet { she / he } might be ____ just a-round the cor - ner

waiting for me. _____

Will I rec - og - nize a

light in {her / his} eyes _ that no oth - er eyes _ re -

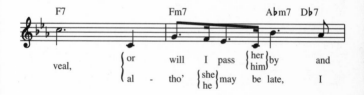

veal, {or will I pass {her / him} by and / al - tho' {she / he} may be late, I}

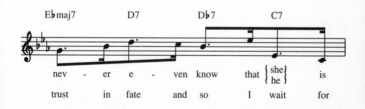

{nev - er e - ven know that {she / he} is / trust in fate and so I wait for}

my i - deal.
my i - deal.

MY ROMANCE
from *JUMBO*

Words by LORENZ HART
Music by RICHARD RODGERS

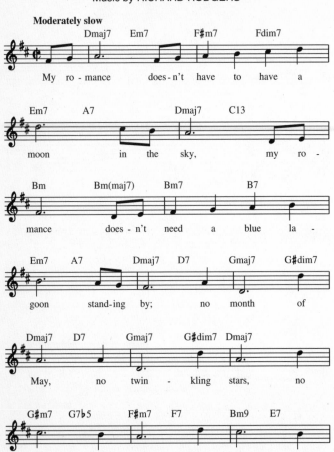

Moderately slow

My ro- mance does- n't have to have a moon in the sky, my ro- mance does- n't need a blue la- goon stand-ing by; no month of May, no twin - kling stars, no hide a - way, no soft gui-

tars.   My ro - mance   does - n't

need a cas - tle ris - ing in

Spain,   nor a dance   to a

con - stant - ly sur - pris - ing re -

frain. Wide a - wake I can make my most fan -

tas - tic dreams come true; my ro - mance does-n't

need a thing but you. _____

NEVERTHELESS
(I'm in Love with You)

Words and Music by BERT KALMAR
and HARRY RUBY

May - be I'm right and may - be I'm wrong, and may - be I'm weak and may - be I'm strong; but nev - er - the - less, I'm in love with you.

May - be I'll win and may - be I'll lose, and may - be I'm in for cry - in' the blues; but nev - er - the - less, I'm in love with you.

ON THE SUNNY SIDE OF THE STREET

Lyric by DOROTHY FIELDS
Music by JIMMY McHUGH

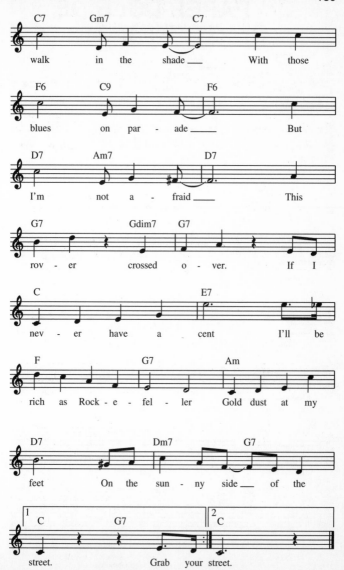

PAPER DOLL

Words and Music by
JOHNNY S. BLACK

I'm goin' to buy a pa-per doll that I can call my own, a doll that oth-er fel-lows can-not steal and then the flir-ty, flir-ty guys with their flir-ty, flir-ty eyes, will have to flirt with dol-lies that are real. When I come home at night she will be wait-ing, __ She'll be the tru-est doll in all this world. I'd rath-er have a pa-per doll to call my own, than have a fick-le-mind-ed real live girl. I'm goin' to girl. __

SOLITUDE

Words and Music by DUKE ELLINGTON,
EDDIE DE LANGE and IRVING MILLS

PENNIES FROM HEAVEN

from PENNIES FROM HEAVEN

Words by JOHN BURKE
Music by ARTHUR JOHNSTON

PICK YOURSELF UP

from SWING TIME

Words by DOROTHY FIELDS
Music by JEROME KERN

Noth - ing's im - pos - si - ble I have found. For when my chin is on the ground I pick my-self up, dust my-self off, start all o - ver a - gain.

Don't lose your con - fi - dence if you slip, be grate - ful for a pleas - ant trip, and pick your-self up, dust your - self off, start all o - ver a - gain.

Work like a soul in - gain.

RED SAILS IN THE SUNSET

Words by JIMMY KENNEDY
Music by HUGH WILLIAMS (WILL GROSZ)

SEPTEMBER SONG

from the Musical Play KNICKERBOCKER HOLIDAY

Words by MAXWELL ANDERSON
Music by KURT WEILL

SOPHISTICATED LADY

Words and Music by DUKE ELLINGTON,
IRVING MILLS and MITCHELL PARISH

Moderately

Bbm7 — They say____ in-to your ear-ly life ro-mance

Gb7 F7 E7 Eb7

Abmaj7 — came,____ and in this heart of yours burned a

Ab7 G7 Gb7 F7

Bb7 — flame,____ a flame that flick-ered one day and

Bbm7 Eb7

Abmaj7 Cm7b5 F7b9 Bbm7 — died a - way. Then,____ with dis - il -

Gb7 F7 E7 Eb7 Abmaj7 — lu - sion deep in your eyes,____ you learned that

Ab7 G7 Gb7 F7 Bb7 — fools in love soon grow wise.____ The years have

Bbm7 Eb7 Abmaj7 Am7b5 D7 — changed you, some-how; I see you now.

SOUTH OF THE BORDER
(Down Mexico Way)

Words and Music by JIMMY KENNEDY
and MICHAEL CARR

The mis-sion bells told me

that I must-n't stay

south of the bor - der

down Mex - i - co way.

Ay! Ay! Ay! Ay!

Ay! Ay! Ay! Ay!

Ay! Ay! Ay! Ay!

Ay! Ay! Ay! Ay!

THE WAY YOU LOOK TONIGHT

from SWING TIME

Words by DOROTHY FIELDS
Music by JEROME KERN

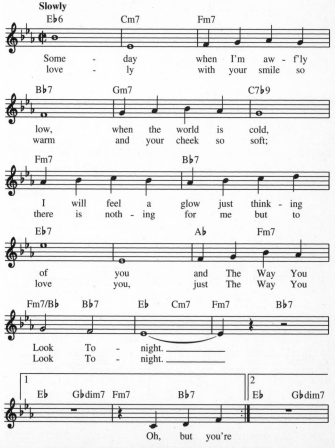

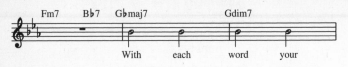

With each word your

ten - der - ness grows, ____

tear - ing my fear ____ a - part, ____

____ and that laugh that

wrin - kles your nose ____

touch - es my fool - ish

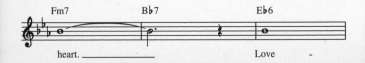

heart. ____ Love -

Cm7   Fm7   Bb9

ly,   nev - er,   nev - er   change,

Gm7   C7b9   Fm7

keep that breath - less charm,   won't you please ar -

Bb7   Eb7

range it. 'Cause I   love   you,

Ab   Fm7   Fm7/Bb   Bb7

just The Way You Look To -

Eb   Cm7   Fm9   Bb9   Ebmaj7   Cm7

night. Mm ___   mm ___   mm, ___

Fm7   Bb7   Ab6   G   Edim7   Fm

mm, ___   just The Way You

Fm7/Bb   Bb7   Eb6

Look To - night. ___

STOMPIN' AT THE SAVOY

Words and Music by BENNY GOODMAN, EDGAR SAMPSON,
CHICK WEBB and ANDY RAZAF

Medium Swing tempo   F

Sa - voy, ____ the home of sweet ro - mance;
____ just like a cling - in' vine, ____

C9   F

Sa - voy, ____ it wins you at a glance;
your lips ____ so warm and sweet as wine, ____

F#dim7   Gm7

Sa - voy, ____ gives hap - py feet a chance.
your cheek ____ so soft and close to mine, ____

C9   [1]   F

to dance. ____
di - vine! ____

[2]   C9   F

Your form ____

F7   Bb7   B7

How my heart is

sing-in' _____ while the band is

swing-in'! _____ Nev - er tired of

romp-in' _____ and stomp-in' with you __

at the Sa - voy. What joy! __ A per-fect hol - i - day!_

__ Sa - voy, __ where we can glide and sway; _

__ Sa - voy, __ there let me stomp a - way_

__ with you. __

STORMY WEATHER
(Keeps Rainin' All the Time)
from COTTON CLUB PARADE OF 1933
Lyric by TED KOEHLER
Music by HAROLD ARLEN

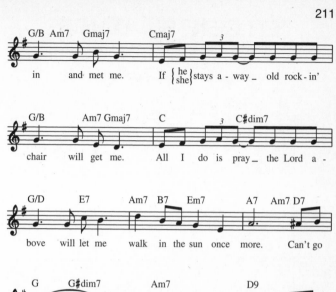

G/B Am7 Gmaj7   Cmaj7   *3*

in   and met me.   If {he/she} stays a - way — old rock - in'

G/B   Am7 Gmaj7   C   *3* C#dim7

chair   will get me.   All I   do is pray — the Lord a -

G/D   E7   Am7   B7   Em7   A7   Am7 D7

bove   will let me   walk in the sun once more.   Can't go

G   G#dim7   Am7   D9

on, _____ ev - 'ry - thing I had is gone, storm - y

G   E7   Am7   D9

weath - er. _____   Since my {man/gal} and I _____ ain't to -

G   E7   Am7   D7#5(b9)   G

geth - er, _____ keeps rain - in' all __ the time. _____

Am7   D7#5(b9)   G   Am7 Abmaj7 Gmaj7 C G6

Keeps rain - in' all __ the time. _____

TEN CENTS A DANCE

from SIMPLE SIMON

Words by LORENZ HART
Music by RICHARD RODGERS

Slowly

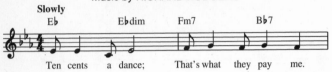

Ten cents a dance; That's what they pay me.

Gosh, how they weigh me down!

Ten cents a dance, pan-sies and rough guys,

tough guys who tear my gown!

Sev-en to mid-night, I hear drums,

loud - ly   the   sax - o - phone   blows,

trum - pets   are   tear - ing   my   ear - drums,

cus - tom - ers crush   my   toes.   Some - times   I think

I've found   my   he - ro,   but it's   a   queer   ro -

mance.   All   that   you   need ___   is   a

tick - et;   Come on,   big   boy,   ten cents a   dance!

THANKS FOR THE MEMORY

from the Paramount Picture BIG BROADCAST OF 1938

Words and Music by LEO ROBIN
and RALPH RAINGER

Moderately

Thanks for the mem-o-ry of can-dle-light and wine,
Thanks for the mem-o-ry of sen-ti-men-tal verse,

cas-tles on the Rhine, the Par-the-non and mo-ments on the
noth-ing in my purse, and chuck-les when the preach-er said, "For

Hud-son Riv-er Line. How love-ly it was!
bet-ter or for worse.". How love-ly it was!

Thanks for the mem-o-ry of rain-y af-ter-noons,
Thanks for the mem-o-ry of lin-ge-rie with lace,

swing-y Har-lem tunes, and mo-tor trips and burn-ing lips and
Pils-ner by the case, and how I jumped the day you trumped my

burn-ing toast and prunes. How love-ly it
one and on-ly ace. How love-ly it

was! Man-y's the time that we feast-ed and
was! We said good-bye with a high-ball; then

Abmaj7 — 3 — — 3 — **Adim7**

man - y's the time that we fast - ed. Oh,
I got as "high" as a stee - ple. But

Cmaj7 **Am7** **Dm7** **G9**

well, it was swell while it last - ed; we
we were in - tel - li - gent peo - ple; no

Gm7 **C7#5** **Gm7** **C7**

did have fun and no harm done. And thanks for the
tears, no fuss, Hur - ray for us. So thanks for the

Fmaj7 **F#dim7**

mem - o - ry of sun - burns at the shore, _
mem - o - ry and strict - ly en - tre - nous, _

C7 **F6** **D7** **Gm7**

nights in Sing - a - pore. _ You might have been a head-ache but you
dar - ling, how are you? _ And how are all the lit - tle dreams that

1
D7 **Gm7** **C7** **F6** **D7b9**

nev - er were a bore, _ so thank you so much.

2
D7 **Gm7** **Abdim7** **Am7**

nev - er did come true? _ Awf - 'ly glad I met you, cheer - i -

Abm7 **Db7** **Gm7** **C9** **F6**

o and too-dle-oo _ and thank you so much!

THEM THERE EYES

Words and Music by MACEO PINKARD,
WILLIAM TRACEY and DORIS TAUBER

217

G9#5
sure start - ed some - thin' with them there
C
C7
eyes,
You'd bet - ter
F
watch them if you're wise.
They spar - kle,
F#dim
C
they bub - ble, they're gon - na get you in a
D7
G9
C
whole lot of trou - ble, You're o - ver-work - in' 'em
1
D7
G7
there's dan - ger lurk - in' in them there
C
2
D7
G7
C
eyes. them there eyes.

THERE'S A SMALL HOTEL

from ON YOUR TOES

Words by LORENZ HART
Music by RICHARD RODGERS

see a dis - tant stee - ple; not a sign of

peo - ple, who wants peo - ple?

When the stee - ple bell says, "Good

night, sleep well," we'll thank the small ho - tel.____ We'll creep in-

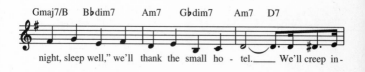

to our lit - tle shell ____ and we will thank the small ho -

tel to - geth - er. _____

THESE FOOLISH THINGS
(Remind Me of You)

Words by HOLT MARVELL
Music by JACK STRACHEY

THIS CAN'T BE LOVE
from THE BOYS FROM SYRACUSE

Words by LORENZ HART
Music by RICHARD RODGERS

Moderately

This Can't Be Love be - cause I

feel so well, ___ no sobs, no sor -

- rows, no sighs; ___

This Can't Be Love, I get no diz - zy spell..

___ My head is not ___ in the

skies, _____ my heart does not stand still, _

_ just hear it beat! This is too

sweet to be

love. This Can't Be Love be - cause I

feel so well; ___ but still I love to look _

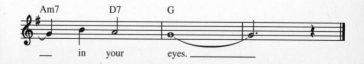

_ in your eyes. _____

TOP HAT,
WHITE TIE AND TAILS

from the RKO Radio Motion Picture TOP HAT

Words and Music by
IRVING BERLIN

I just got an in - vi - ta - tion through the mails. ____

____ "Your pres - ence re - quest - ed this

eve - ning, it's for - mal." A top hat, a white tie and

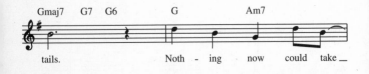

tails. Noth - ing now could take ____

____ the wind out of my sails, _____ be -

cause I'm in - vit - ed to step out this eve - ning with

top hat and white tie and tails.

I'm _____ put - tin' on my

top hat, _____ ty - in' up my

white tie, _____ brush - in' off my

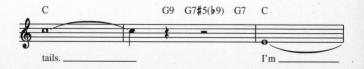

tails. _____ I'm _____

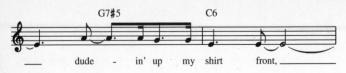

dude - in' up my shirt front, _____

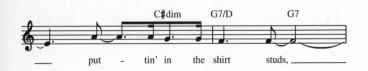

put - tin' in the shirt studs, _____

pol - ish-in' my nails. _____ I'm step - pin'

out, my dear, to breathe _ an at - mos - phere

that sim - ply reeks with class. _____

And I trust that you'll _

ex - cuse my dust when I step on the

gas. For I'll be there, _____

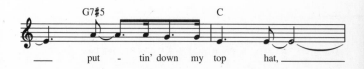

_____ put - tin' down my top hat, _____

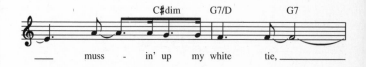

_____ muss - in' up my white tie, _____

_____ danc - in' in my tails. _____

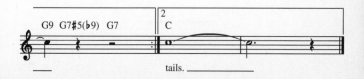

_____ tails. _____

TWO SLEEPY PEOPLE

from the Paramount Motion Picture
THANKS FOR THE MEMORY

Words by FRANK LOESSER
Music by HOAGY CARMICHAEL

Here we are, out of cig-a-rettes,___
Here we are, in the co-zy chair,___

hold-ing hands and yawn-ing,
pick-ing on a wish-bone

look how late it gets.___ Two sleep-y peo-ple, by
from the Frig-id-aire,___ Two sleep-y peo-ple with

dawn's ear-ly light, and too much in love to say "Good
noth-ing to say and

night." too much in love to break a-

way. Do you re-mem-ber the nights we used to

lin-ger in the hall? ___

THE VERY THOUGHT OF YOU

Words and Music by
RAY NOBLE

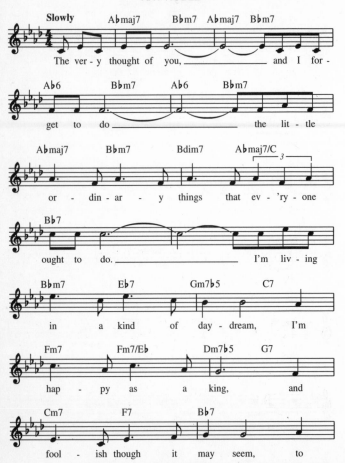

Slowly

The ver-y thought of you, _____ and I for-get to do _____ the lit-tle or-din-ar — y things that ev-'ry-one ought to do. _____ I'm liv-ing in a kind of day-dream, I'm hap-py as a king, and fool-ish though it may seem, to

WHAT A DIFF'RENCE A DAY MADE

English Words by STANLEY ADAMS
Music and Spanish Words by MARIA GREVER

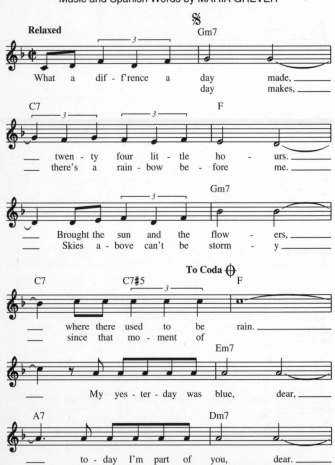

What a dif-f'rence a day made,
day makes,
twen-ty four lit-tle ho - urs.
there's a rain-bow be - fore me.
Brought the sun and the flow - ers,
Skies a-bove can't be storm - y
where there used to be rain.
since that mo-ment of
My yes-ter-day was blue, dear,
to-day I'm part of you, dear.

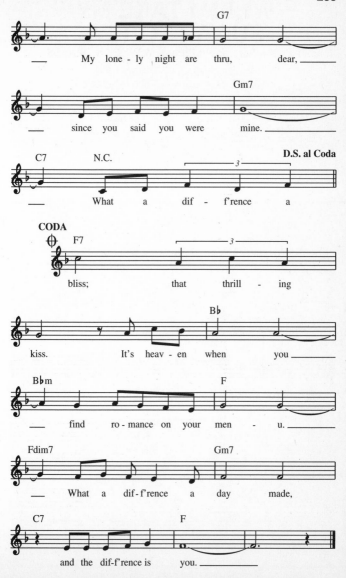

WHEN I TAKE MY SUGAR TO TEA

from the Paramount Picture MONKEY BUSINESS

Words and Music by SAMMY FAIN,
IRVING KAHAL and PIERRE NORMAN

we for-get a-bout our cares, ___

rub - bing el - bows at the Ritz ___

with those mil - lion - aires. _____ When I

take my sug - ar to tea, ___ I'm as

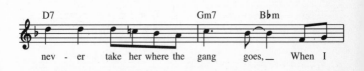

Ritz - y as I can be, _____ 'cause I

nev - er take her where the gang goes, _ When I

take my sug - ar to tea.

WHERE OR WHEN
from BABES IN ARMS

Words by LORENZ HART
Music by RICHARD RODGERS

Dm7b5   G7   Cm   Fm7

____ Some things that hap - pen for the

Dm7   G7   Dm7   G7   Cm

first time, _____ seem to be

Fm7   Cm7   F7   Fm7   Bb7

hap - pen - ing a - gain. _____

Eb   Eb6   Ebmaj7

And so it seems that we have met be -

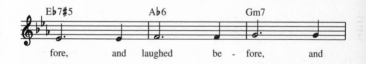

Eb7#5   Ab6   Gm7

fore, and laughed be - fore, and

Fm7   Gm7   C7   Fm7

loved be - fore, but who knows

Bb7   Bb7b9   Eb6   Abm   Eb

When Or When! _____

WHERE THE BLUE
OF THE NIGHT
(Meets the Gold of the Day)

Lyric and Music by FRED E. AHLERT,
BING CROSBY and ROY TURK

Moderately

Where the blue of the night meets the

gold of the day. Some - one

waits for me._____ And the

gold of her hair crowns the blue of her

eyes like a ha - lo, ten - der -

ly._____ If on - ly

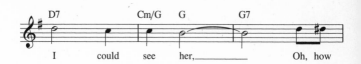

I could see her,_____ Oh, how

hap - py I would be!_____

__ Where the blue of the night meets the

gold of the day. Some - one waits for

me._____ Where the me._____

WRAP YOUR TROUBLES IN DREAMS
(And Dream Your Troubles Away)

Lyric by TED KOEHLER and BILLY MOLL
Music by HARRY BARRIS

Moderately slow

When skies are cloud-y and gray, they're on-ly gray for a day, So wrap your trou-bles in dreams and dream your trou-bles a-way. Un-til that sun-shine peeps thru, there's on-ly one thing to do, just wrap your trou-bles in dreams and dream your trou-bles a-way. Your

YOU ARE TOO BEAUTIFUL

from HALLELUJAH, I'M A BUM

Words by LORENZ HART
Music by RICHARD RODGERS

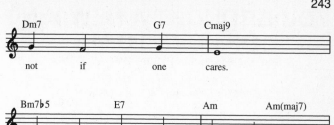

not   if   one   cares.

Have   you   been   com - par - ing

my   ev - 'ry   kiss   with   theirs?

If   on   the   oth - er   hand   I'm   faith - ful   to   you,   it's

not   through   a   sense   of   du - ty.

You   are   too   beau - ti - ful   and   I   am   a   fool   for

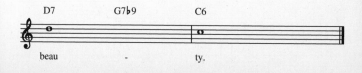

beau   -   ty.

YOU BROUGHT A NEW KIND OF LOVE TO ME

from the Paramount Picture THE BIG POND

Words and Music by SAMMY FAIN,
IRVING KAHAL and PIERRE NORMAN

YOU OUGHTA BE IN PICTURES

Words and Music by DANA SUESSE and EDWARD HEYMAN

Moderately

You ough-ta be in pic-tures, ___
Your voice would thrill a na-tion, ___

You're won-der-ful to see,
Your face would be a-dored,

You ough-ta be in pic-tures, ___ Oh
You'd make a great sen-sa-tion ___ With

what a hit ___ you would be! ___
wealth and fame ___

your re-ward; ___ And if you should

kiss the way ___ you kiss,

when we are all a - lone, ___

You'd make ev - 'ry girl and man ___ a fan

wor - ship - ing at your throne. ___

You ough - ta shine as bright - ly ___

As Ju - pi - ter and Mars;

You ough - ta be in pic - tures, ___ My

star of stars!

YOU'RE MY EVERYTHING

Lyric by MORT DIXON and JOE YOUNG
Music by HARRY WARREN

Slowly, with much expression

YOURS
(Cuando se Quiere de Veras)

Words by ALBERT GAMSE and JACK SHERR
Music by GONZALO ROIG

Dreamily

Yours till the stars lose their glo-ry! Yours till the birds fail to sing! Yours to the end of life's sto-ry, this pledge to you, dear, I bring!

Yours in ___ the gray of ___ De-
cem - ber ___

B7

here or ___ on far dis - tant

Em

shores! ___ I've nev - er

A7   D7   B7

loved an - y - one the way ___ I love

Em   B7   Em

you!   How   could   I?

Gm   D

When I was born to be ___

A7   D

___ just yours. ___

GUITAR CHORD FRAMES

	C	Cm	C+	C6	Cm6
C					

	C#	C#m	C#+	C#6	C#m6
C#/Db					

	D	Dm	D+	D6	Dm6
D					

	Eb	Ebm	Eb+	Eb6	Ebm6
Eb/D#					

	E	Em	E+	E6	Em6
E					

	F	Fm	F+	F6	Fm6
F					

This guitar chord reference includes 120 commonly used
chords. For a more complete guide to guitar chords, see
"THE PAPERBACK CHORD BOOK" (HL00702009).

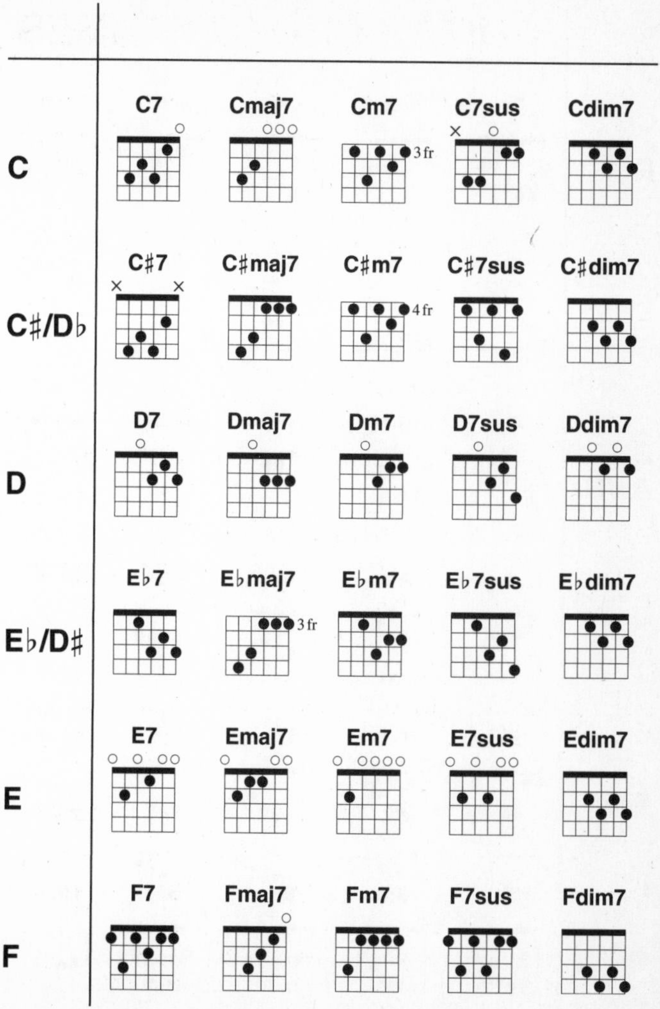
C
C7
Cmaj7
Cm7
3 fr
C7sus
Cdim7
C♯/D♭
C♯7
C♯maj7
C♯m7
4 fr
C♯7sus
C♯dim7
D
D7
Dmaj7
Dm7
D7sus
Ddim7
E♭/D♯
E♭7
E♭maj7
3 fr
E♭m7
E♭7sus
E♭dim7
E
E7
Emaj7
Em7
E7sus
Edim7
F
F7
Fmaj7
Fm7
F7sus
Fdim7

254

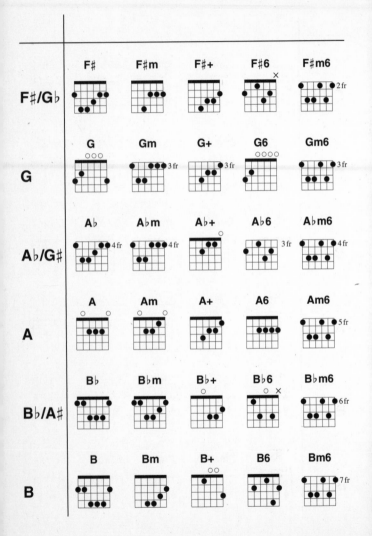

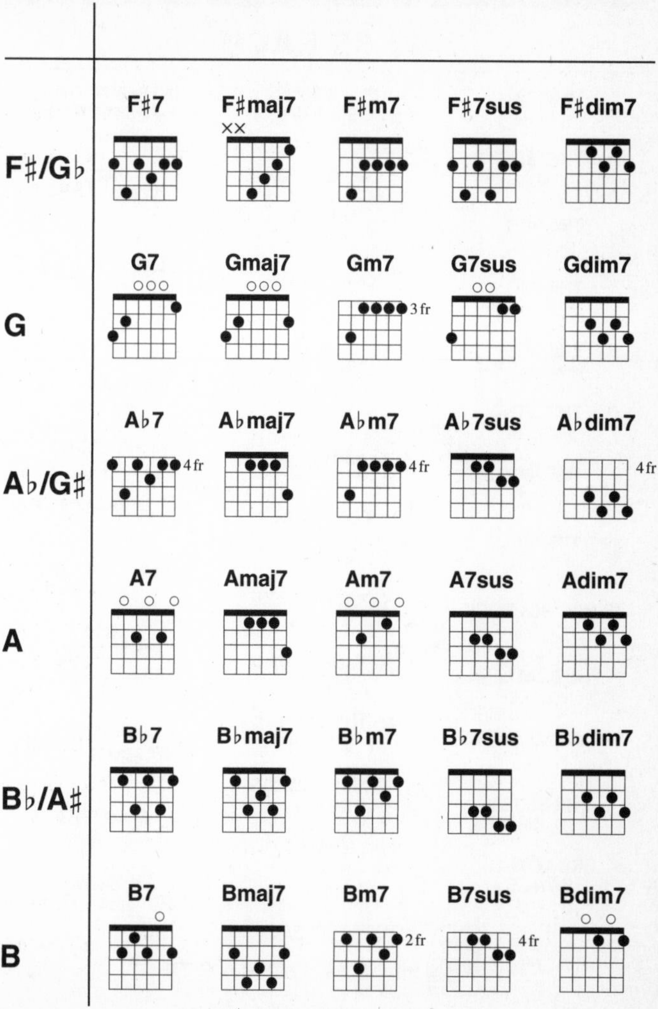
F♯/G♭
F♯7
F♯maj7
F♯m7
F♯7sus
F♯dim7
G
G7
Gmaj7
Gm7
3 fr
G7sus
Gdim7
A♭/G♯
A♭7
4 fr
A♭maj7
A♭m7
4 fr
A♭7sus
A♭dim7
4 fr
A
A7
Amaj7
Am7
A7sus
Adim7
B♭/A♯
B♭7
B♭maj7
B♭m7
B♭7sus
B♭dim7
B
B7
Bmaj7
Bm7
2 fr
B7sus
4 fr
Bdim7

THE PAPERBACK SONGS SERIES

$7.95 EACH

THE '20s
00240236

THE '30s
00240238

THE '40s
00240239

THE '50s
00240240

THE '60s
00240241

THE '70s
00240242

THE '80s
00240243

THE '90s
00240244

'80s & '90s ROCK
00240126

THE BEATLES
00702008

BIG BAND SWING
00240171

THE BLUES
00702014

BROADWAY SONGS
00240157

CHILDREN'S SONGS
00240149

CHORDS FOR KEYBOARD & GUITAR
00702009

CHRISTMAS CAROLS
00240142

CHRISTMAS SONGS
00240208

CLASSIC ROCK
00310058

CLASSICAL THEMES
00240160

COUNTRY HITS
00702013

NEIL DIAMOND
00702012

GOOD OL' SONGS
00240159

GOSPEL SONGS
00240143

HYMNS
00240103

INTERNATIONAL FOLKSONGS
00240104

JAZZ STANDARDS
00240114

LATIN SONGS
00240156

LOVE SONGS
00240150

MOTOWN HITS
00240125

MOVIE MUSIC
00240113

POP/ROCK
00240179

ELVIS PRESLEY
00240102

THE ROCK & ROLL COLLECTION
00702020

RODGERS & HAMMERSTEIN
00240177

SOUL HITS
00240178

TV THEMES
00240170

FOR MORE INFORMATION, SEE YOUR LOCAL MUSIC DEALER,
OR WRITE TO:

HAL•LEONARD®
C O R P O R A T I O N
7777 W. BLUEMOUND RD. P.O. BOX 13819 MILWAUKEE, WI 53213

www.halleonard.com